Peregrinatio: Poems for Antarctica

Peregrinatio: Poems for Antarctica

by

Gloria Heffernan

© 2023 Gloria Heffernan. All rights reserved.
This material may not be reproduced in any form, published,
reprinted, recorded, performed, broadcast,
rewritten or redistributed without
the explicit permission of Gloria Heffernan.
All such actions are strictly prohibited by law.

Cover design by Shay Culligan
Cover image by James M. Heffernan
Author photo by James M. Heffernan

ISBN: 978-1-63980-349-1

Library of Congress Control Number: 2023941654

Kelsay Books
502 South 1040 East, A-119
American Fork, Utah 84003
Kelsaybooks.com

For Jim:
To the ends of the earth
and back.

Other Books by Gloria Heffernan

Exploring Poetry of Presence: A Companion Guide for Readers, Writers, and Workshop Facilitators (Back Porch Productions)

What the Gratitude List Said to the Bucket List (New York Quarterly Books)

Some of Our Parts (Finishing Line Press)

Hail to the Symptom (Moonstone Press)

Peregrinatio: Poems for Antarctica was a finalist in the Grayson Chapbook Competition.

Acknowledgments

Thank you to the editors of the following publications for publishing the following works:

Canary: "Call of the Krill," "Nightmare on Ice"

Caring for Creation: St. Andrew's Episcopal Church 2022 Poetry Contest Anthology: "Entreaty"

Dappled Things: "Peregrinatio"

Feral: "Beacon at the Bottom of the World"

Galway Review: "The World Without Us"

Raw Arts Review: "Deception Island," "Expedition Antarctica"

Contents

Entreaty	19
Voyage to Antarctica	20
Drake Passage	21
Love at First Site	22
Peregrinatio	23
Call of the Krill	25
The Tender Boat	27
Borrowed Boots	29
The Washing of Feet	30
The Obligatory Penguin Poem	31
Emperors of Ice	32
Half-Moon Island	33
Frozen	34
Deception Island	35
Hektor Whaling Station	36
Reliquary at Whaler's Bay	37
Expedition Antarctica	38
The Gift Shop Is Now Open	42
Polar Abecedarian	44
Nightmare on Ice	45
Loving the Skua	46
Rocking the Boat	48
The Captain's Portrait	50
Blue	52
A Day Without a Camera	53
Sonnet for a Nameless Iceberg	54
At Sea	55
Beacon at the Bottom of the World	57
Rookery, The Falklands	58
Inventory	60
Core Values	61
To Dream of Antarctica	62
The World Without Us	63
Treaty	64

Writing Antarctica

A land that defies language,
but inspires poetry,
a land that leaves you speechless
but dares you to tell the tale.

A Sacred Journey

The word *peregrinatio* is translated from the Latin as "a sacred journey." My husband Jim and I didn't know that we were embarking on such a journey when we traveled to Antarctica in 2019. We both believed it would be the oft-touted "trip of a lifetime," and it did indeed live up to that expectation. But it also left me with lingering questions about what it means to set foot on that continent. The trip engendered a feeling of duty and stewardship that I can only repay with poetry. I have been working on this book ever since.

While writing these poems, I have been haunted by Wendell Berry's lines in "How to Be a Poet":

> There are no unsacred places;
> there are only sacred places
> and desecrated places.

My prayer is that Antarctica will never become one of those desecrated places.

In 1959, the Antarctic Treaty was signed by twelve nations declaring that "Antarctica shall be used for peaceful purposes only. There shall be prohibited . . . any measures of a military nature, such as the establishment of military bases and fortifications, the carrying out of military maneuvers, as well as the testing of any type of weapons." This treaty now has fifty-four signatory nations which have chosen cooperation and peace over political power and exploitation of natural resources. While the treaty has its flaws, it is unparalleled as a model of international cooperation.

Nonetheless, as far-reaching as the Antarctic Treaty is, it could not anticipate the many threats the future would hold for the seventh continent. Today, this remote corner of the world attracts an average of 75,000 tourists a year and the number is growing. The International Association of Antarctica Tour Operators (IAATO), founded in 1991, works to "advocate and promote the practice of safe and environmentally responsible private-sector travel to the Antarctic." This cooperative council of tour operators places limits on the number of tourists allowed to land at any site, maintains strict guidelines regarding the safety of wildlife and imposes fines and penalties on tour operators who do not adhere to these policies.

IAATO's mission is to foster appreciation, education and commitment to conservation among visitors to Antarctica. Under its rigorous guidelines, tour operators are urged to stress educational programming as an integral part of their offerings. Member tour operators are also required to enforce conservation protocols to protect the environment. These measures have been effective so far and have protected Antarctica from the fate of places like Mount Everest, Machu Pichu, and our own national parks where little has been done to deter overcrowding, pollution, and what Wendell Berry would most certainly deem desecration.

But as I traveled the breathtaking coastal waters on a state-of-the-art, environmentally responsible cruise ship and listened to the daily lectures delivered by distinguished scientists, and hiked the vast, untouched landscape, and maintained my requisite fifteen-foot distance from all wildlife, I couldn't help feeling that I was trespassing on sacred ground.

The questions linger. How can tourism and conservation co-exist? Does first-hand experience truly inspire advocacy and stewardship of our wildest places? Will the coldest place on Earth simply become the hottest new destination? And most troubling on a personal level, was I an accomplice in the possible desecration of this unique and vital place?

I don't presume to have the answers. In these poems, I try to explore the questions: the risks, the rewards, and the profound privilege of setting foot on this very sacred ground.

Gloria Heffernan
Syracuse, NY
March 2023

Entreaty

In the end we will conserve only what we love;
We will love only what we understand;
And we will understand only what we have been taught.
—Baba Dioum

Who am I to teach of Antarctica?
Who am I to say, *Love this place*?
Who am I to plead
for a land so few will ever see?

I am a witness.
I am a trespasser.
I am one of a privileged few who has walked
in the company of the Gentoo penguin
that hasn't yet learned to fear our kind.

I am a messenger,
back from the bottom of the world
and like Orpheus,
I can't help but look back
at that which I love
and fear will disappear.

I am a pilgrim,
Praying for the coldest place on Earth.
Praying that it will remain cold.
Praying that its creatures will prevail.
Praying that the land I love
will be safe from the likes of me.

Voyage to Antarctica

You depart from Ushuaia,
capital of Tierra del Fuego,
the southernmost tip
of South America
at the foot of the Andes—
the beginning of a five-day voyage
through riotous waves
and shrieking winds
that scream in your ears,

> *Are you sure*
> *this is where you meant to go?*

Gradually, you succumb
to the spinning head
and churning stomach,
and the fear that perhaps
this was a mistake after all.

So you retreat to your cabin,
close your eyes
and pray for respite
from the gyrating seas.

And as you surrender,
the ship carries you
through the turmoil
until you finally sigh and say,

> *Yes . . .*
> *This is the place.*

Drake Passage

Turbulent borderline between continents
where the Atlantic and Pacific collide,
Gatekeeper of Antarctica,
exact your toll.

Blow with Wagnerian winds.
Pelt us with torrents of sleet.
Stipple our cheeks with frozen shrapnel
if we foolishly try to step into your gales.

Taunt us when we stumble down
the lurching corridors of the massive ship
you pitch to the peak of forty-foot waves
then drop into the trough below.

Laugh at us as we crouch in our cabins
clutching our bellies in narrow beds.
If you find us weak and wanting,
as you no doubt will, demand more.

The fare we've paid is no paltry thing
but we cannot bribe you with mere money.
Prove that despite our daring illusions,
we are defenseless in your grip.

Love at First Site

After two blustery days at sea,
we know we are approaching land
long before we hear the announcement.

We have been watching Arctic Terns circling
since sunrise urging us up to the deck
for our first sight of the South Shetland Islands.

The birds race to the ship—
Are they here to guide us to shore?
Of course not.

They are merely flying to the stern
to feast in the churn
that drives today's catch to the surface.

But I tell myself the story
that they are a welcoming committee
deployed by the colony of penguins

huddled together on the beach
chattering as if they had known all along
that we were on our way,

and eager to see our faces as we catch
our first glimpse of their glittering
world of snow and sky and ice.

Peregrinatio

My family crest depicts a whale
gliding west across the sea.
Is this the whale that sheltered St. Brendan
and his monks on their ancient voyage?

Today I am the voyager
perched on a rubber boat in the Southern Ocean,
one of a dozen onlookers gazing at a Humpback whale
as she glides silently through the waves
then disappears

only to resurface moments later
close enough to touch—though I don't dare.
But I wonder what she would do
if I slid silently over the side.

Would she invite me to board her broad back
like her ancestor who welcomed those monks?
When Brendan prayed for a miracle,
God sent a leviathan disguised as an island.

Is she my island as she resurfaces
emitting a sound deeper than the ocean—
a sonorous exhalation echoing the winds
that drove the monks across the Atlantic?

We are held in the rhythm of that breath—
embraced by the holy silence that surrounds it.
She pauses as if calling us to prayer
and in concert we all exhale as one.

In the stillness that follows,
I think of those monks
and imagine their sense of wonder
when the island on which they perched
issued forth such a breath.

As she disappears beneath the waves
I ponder my place in that ancient tradition—
peregrinatio,
the sacred voyage into the unknown
where miracles still abound.

Call of the Krill

They move as one
across the Southern Ocean
in swarms a billion strong,
a mile wide.
Shimmering islands
swimming beneath the waves.

No, they are not the creatures
that lure you to Antarctica
with their majesty and grace.
But they lure the Humpback whales
who travel 5,000 miles
just to feast on them.

Tiny krill, miraculous in their way.
Each less than an ounce on its own.
Combined, a population
that outweighs all of humanity
for the brief Austral summer.

They are the unwitting partners
in the Humpbacks' intricate choreography
as the whales plunge below the surface,
one leader submerging far into the deep
piercing the silence with its song,
signaling its kin to swirl
in synchronized spirals,
erecting walls of bubbles
the frenzied krill cannot or will not penetrate.

And then the gorging
as leviathans break the surface
open-mouthed,

consuming their prey by the ton,
enough in one season
to sustain them for the year ahead.

The synergy of supply and demand,
monumental and miniscule.
All held in place by one point
on the thermometer as the ocean warms.
When we mourn the loss of the whales,
who will remember the krill that fed them
silent and unseen?

The Tender Boat

Haibun for an Antarctic Voyage

They call them Tender Boats. Rubber vessels built to carry passengers from ship to shore and back. Small and sturdy, surprisingly stable. Built to gallop over choppy waves. I don't know how the vessel got its name, and yet, when I recall those transports speeding over open water, it is tenderness that overwhelms me.

The tender boat rocks.
Waves dip and drive us to shore.
Every swell a heartbeat.

We board them from the Tender Pit. Deep in the cavernous bay of the ship where passengers may not venture on their own. Huddled in a narrow hallway, sweltering in parkas and mittens we file down slippery steel steps to the loading platform. Once settled into the small boat, we feel the vastness of the ship at our backs.

We descend the stairs.
Emerge into the cold air like babes
leaving the warm womb.

The ride is fast and rough. No belts or benches, we lean against rubber bumpers, hold fast to ropes threaded along the sides, and still insist on snapping photos one-handed as the boat lurches crazily like a cork in the rolling waves. How many cameras litter the floor of Paradise Bay taking pictures of penguins' bellies?

Penguins never pose.
Seals have no use for selfies.
Forget your camera.

As we come ashore, a new tenderness. A visceral awe that begins in the pit of my stomach and overwhelms my senses as I pass a pair of drowsy seals huddled together on the beach and catch sight of a Humpback whale breaching in the distance.

I store memories
in the gold seamed tender pit
where reverence resides.

Borrowed Boots

I am the pair of ship-issued boots
that you will wear in the coldest place on earth.
I am a safeguard against cross-contamination
as we travel the Antarctic peninsula,
and a guarantee that no one leaves the ship
shoddily shod.

Think of me as the library book
that will tell you a story
beyond your wildest imaginings
before you return me to the shelf.

Yes, I have heard it all . . .
They're so ugly, too heavy,
Don't they come in a different color?
I forgive you. And to prove it,
I will save your life every day of this journey.
I will keep you warm and dry and sure-footed
as you trek treacherous trails covered in snow,
and wander windblown plains where no trail exists.

Cinderella's glass slippers had nothing on me.
True, you won't wear me to waltz in a grand ballroom,
but Cinderella never climbed an Antarctic hillside to watch
a Wandering Albatross glide over the Southern Ocean.
And as for Prince Charming, his whole kingdom
can't come close to where I will take you.

I will be your closest companion.
I will carry your sole in my hands.
By the end of this voyage,
you will beg me to come home with you.
You will offer any price
to stow me in your luggage.
But just like the land I will carry you through,
I am not for sale.

The Washing of Feet

Just a simple sanitation procedure.
To re-enter the ship, you must go through
the boot washing station.
Step up onto the platform,
set your feet on the spinning wire brushes.
Hold on as the machine squeezes and scours
the soles and shafts of your boots,
expelling mud and penguin poop
from every tread and seam.

Next comes the disinfectant rinse
to eliminate any lingering microorganism
that might threaten a penguin colony
on a neighboring island.
When your soles have been cleansed,
you may proceed.

Each day, the process evolves—
Procedure becomes ritual.
Ritual becomes sacrament.
When Jesus knelt before his apostles
to wash their feet, he said,
*"You do not realize now what I am doing,
but later you will understand."*

Later you will understand
this ritual cleansing is a sacred compact
with Antarctica and her inhabitants.
This is not about housekeeping.
This is about salvation.
This is not about risk management.
This is about honoring fragility.
This is not about clean boots.
This is about walking on sacred ground.

The Obligatory Penguin Poem

Okay, let's just get it out of the way.
They are impossibly cute.
Perhaps the hardest thing
about walking the beach at Half-Moon Island
is fighting the urge to pick one up
and snuggle it like a stuffed animal
(regardless of what it might have
to say about the embrace).

And yes, they do stink.
There is no getting away from it
even though I chafe at the complaints
of pampered tourists (like me)
who whine about the odor
that clings to their red parkas
and borrowed boots.

And sure,
they are a noisy lot, gabbling incessantly
with an urgency that suggests
they do indeed have a message for us
if only we would put down our cameras
long enough to listen.

Oh, so easy to sentimentalize,
to romanticize
to anthropomorphize,
to close our eyes
to the fact that our very presence here
is a threat to their existence
no matter how hard we try
to rationalize.

Emperors of Ice

after Wallace Stevens . . . sort of

Not the emperor of ice cream
but surely the emperors of ice
and wind and the dark Austral night.

Yes, their horny feet do protrude,
showing how cold they are,
but no, they are not dumb.

What they can teach us of survival
is more than all the emperors
past or to come.

Could mighty Caesar incubate an egg
through months of Antarctic cold?
I think not.

Nor could Constantine
match the majesty with which these Emperors
endure the privations at the bottom of the world.

And what of Caligula's concupiscent crowds?
What would they do in colonies
 of monogamous mates?

What good are royal garments of black and white
offset with golden collars
if everyone is wearing them?

Did no one brief these birdbrains
on their imperial duties?
Can they even be called Emperors
if they destroy nothing?

Half-Moon Island

If I am honest about it,
I am trespassing here.

This place does not belong to me,
nor any other human.

The trail I navigate clumsily
in borrowed muck boots

is an undulating ribbon
trod into the snow and ice

by generations of Chinstrap Penguins
waddling in single file

from the sea to the rocky crags
of this crater-like dot

in the roiling Southern Ocean.
It is their home.

Pristine water, clean air,
legions of seabirds and seals.

A place undisturbed
until I and my tribe make landfall.

Intruders or pilgrims—
the Chinstraps want to know.

Frozen

I would like to tell you I that was afraid
standing twenty feet from the two fur seals
pounding their chests into each other,
roaring like engines revving up
for a demolition derby.

I would like to tell you that it was not foolish
to stand frozen in place on the beach
when I should have known better
than to linger fumbling with my camera,
heedless of the danger.

I would like to tell you that I had the good sense
to get out of the way instead of gaping
at what might have been two siblings at play
or a territorial battle for this beach where
they were once hunted to the brink of extinction.

What I can tell you is that on this remote island
where I am, at best, an observer,
or at worst, an unwitting threat to their habitat,
these two seals went about their business,
completely oblivious to my presence.

Deception Island

The caldera's warm water
meets the freezing air
in a steamy tango.
We are walking
on the grave of a volcano
that is only playing dead.

The beach is a museum
of decomposition where
the odor of digested fish
lingers in the air—
a distant echo of the stench
of slaughtered whales
hauled onto this shore,
stripped of their flesh,
their fat rendered into oil,
their bones left to litter the beach
like toppled headstones.

Petrels perch on the bleached hulls
of abandoned wooden boats.
Apparitions loom up ahead in the mist—
perhaps the ghosts of whalers
serving penance for their part
in the genocide.

Hektor Whaling Station

1912–1931

The smell of rotting fish permeates
the air around the empty oil tanks towering
over the beach on Deception Island.
Not just any oil. Whale oil.
They called the tanks Digesters.
Three times the height of the bunkhouses
where 200 men manned the station
and hauled the carcasses and stripped the flesh
and rendered the fat of 5,000 whales a year.

Steam rises over the volcanic island
where the warm water of the caldera
collides with the frigid Antarctic air.
Above it all, the russet tanks
loom over the landscape like
something that crash landed
from another planet.

At the other end of the station,
white wooden crosses,
     a dozen or so,
commemorate the whalers
who died there.

For the slaughtered whales,
     half a million or so,
the only monument is bleached bones
frozen on the beach, and this assortment of
hollow carcasses of rusted metal—
a historic site commemorating
the glory days of Antarctic whaling.

Reliquary at Whaler's Bay

The wooden boat, battered by a century of wind,
lies abandoned on the shore of Deception Island,
its bow pointing to Whaler's Bay with palpable longing.

Bleached to the color of a leaden sky,
it smells of sulfur and dead fish,
a dining table for seals and gulls.

The wooden boat is the prone body of an ancient uncle
laid out for viewing on the kitchen table of a cottage
where the wind keens like mourners at an Irish wake.

Constellations of starfish wash up on black sand,
reminding the boat of nights long ago when the sky glittered
while whales sang their hypnotic songs unaware of their fate.

The boat is little more than reclaimed driftwood now. It is
a decaying memory of utility and grace in the service
of destruction. It is a shrine to the commerce of murder.

The boat is not a monument to daring sea men
braving the elements on a volcanic island
near the bottom of the world.

It is a monument to nature's eventual triumph over greed,
a remnant of the industry of death, abandoned
after the volcano finally roared *Enough!*

leaving behind a reliquary on the shore,
frozen in mist, and wind, and time.

Expedition Antarctica

I.   The Trek

Damoy Hut radiates
like a turquoise pendant in the snow.
The bright color,
more than a decorative statement,
is a beacon in the stark white landscape.

We see it from a mile away
Much as the airmen who stopped here
to rest and refuel might have seen it
half a century ago.
A solitary dot in the distance.

The morning sky is heavy with snow.
Sudden whiteouts propel us
into a state of confusion
where earth and sky
collide on a blank canvas
devoid of all but the distant outline
of that single landmark.

A Skua soars above our heads
telling us literally which end is up.
How does she stay aloft
in this wind that chafes
whatever skin isn't covered
by scarves and goggles?

We plant our poles deep into the snow
pulling ourselves forward against the wind.
I marvel to feel sweat trickle down my back
despite the penetrating chill.

II.   Arrival

Approaching the hut,
the first thing we see
is the hefty black kettle
framed in the window,
centered above a single burner.

I imagine the sight of its small flame
flickering under a leaden sky.
How far it would radiate into the darkness
with its promise of comfort
whispered into the roaring wind.

When we reach the hut,
stacked high on cinderblocks
it offers a homey welcome
with its unpainted plywood walls,
and provisions lining the shelves—
tinned peaches, sardines,
salt and flour preserved for fifty years
since the last flight departed.

In the bunk room twelve beds
stacked two-deep
where weary pilots rested
before continuing on to
Port Lockroy to the south.

What did they see
as they wrestled their planes
onto the ice for those brief stopovers?
Always a pass-through,
the hut meant refueling,

a warm meal,
a blanket,
and always in the window
that kettle of boiling water for tea.

III.   Return

Our hike here has been long,
a test of our own endurance,
but a test taken
under the watchful eyes
of expedition leaders
who lay out the safest trail,
who track the weather patterns
to make sure the white-outs,
though briefly blinding,
will pass in due course.
They keep track of our red parkas
as we hobble through drifts.
And even accommodate each request
to snap a picture when we arrive at the hut.

We play at danger,
knowing that after our mile-long trek
back to the landing boat,
windburned, and wet,
exhausted but exhilarated,
we will return to our tastefully appointed ship,
shed our life jackets and boots,
and retire to the upper deck
for afternoon tea poured
not from a black iron kettle,
but a silver tea service
beside a tray of pastries.

Yes, there will be sore feet and aching backs
and raucous exchanges about the gale force winds
that nearly blew us into the churning waters of Dorian Bay.
But we can never know the relief of those pilots,
navigating through an impermeable wall of white
with no horizon to delineate earth from sky
as they crossed the threshold into that
humble hut in the middle
of what some would call
nowhere.

The Gift Shop Is Now Open

If one more passenger tells me how lucky I am, I will—

The tee shirts are $35.00.

    No I won't.
    I won't tell them how my feet ache
    after twelve hours at this cash register.
    I won't tell them that while they were puking
    in their stateroom with the heated floors,
    I was here dizzy on Dramamine because
     nobody cares if I am seasick—
    as long as the doors open on time.

The postcards are a dollar a piece or twelve for ten.

    Yes, I am lucky.
    Lucky to have a job working seven days a week,
    six months out of the year for not much more
    than you paid for this cruise.
    Lucky to Skype with my kids once a week
    while passengers like you complain
    about the lousy internet connection.

The stuffed penguins are on sale today—20% percent off.
Why not buy two? Your grandkids will love them.

    Lucky my mother can take care of my babies
    while I sail around the world in the bunkroom
    I share with two waitresses and one of those
    invisible cleaning ladies who works
    the nightshift so the carpet in the bar
    where you spilled your whiskey sour last night
    won't be stained when you come back
    for another drink tonight.

Will that be cash or charge?

> Lucky your insatiable desire for overpriced souvenirs
> keeps you coming back for more day after day,
> as if you need proof that you were really here
> because memories fade but a shiny Antarctica water bottle
> will last forever . . . in the landfill.

Yes, I am very lucky to be here every day. Thank you. Come again.

Polar Abecedarian

Antarctica
Belongs only to itself,
Cataclysmic and cathartic,
Destructive and dynamic,
Endlessly enshrined in
Frozen fire
Glinting in the heart of the glaciers.
Hear the harmony of wind and ocean.
Ice inspires the stars to glisten ever brighter.
Jagged mountains born of volcanoes serrate the horizon.
Kaleidoscopic visions of the Aurora Australis
Light the sky in
Midwinter when
No one ventures
Over the plains of snow but the Emperor
Penguins and their chicks huddled
Quietly in the pervasive darkness,
Resolutely waiting for their mates to return and
Save them from starvation.
Treacherous winds blast shorelines with icy shrapnel.
Under even these bleakest of conditions,
Visions of unspeakable beauty abound.
Weddell seals wintering beneath the ice rise to
X-ray the horizon through holes on the surface then
Yield again to the coldest water on earth where
Zero degrees feels warmer than a zephyr breeze.

Nightmare on Ice

I wake in the middle of the night
shivering from a dream of Antarctica—
Not shivering from dream images
of a windswept snowscape.

This is the dream where
oil spreads like a bruise over the sea
while a ruptured cruise ship
hemorrhages black ooze
into Neko Harbor.

This is the dream where
tourists trade their mittens and hats
for sunscreen and shorts
as temperatures rise
like a fever across the continent.

This is the dream where I pray
to wake up before the sludge
seeps below the ice shrouding
every creature in viscous muck.

Loving the Skua

or How I Learned I Could Never Be an Ornithologist

On her own, she is attractive enough—
a dark figure soaring across
a glittering white landscape,
dusky wings slicing the polar wind.

A not unlovely sight
until she plunges into a colony
of penguins huddled
along the rocky shoreline.

Plundering the nearest nest,
her scissored beak grasps
the neck of a Gentoo chick
while the desperate mother shrieks
and flaps her flightless wings.
Despite her alarm call,
the other penguins steer clear,
protecting their own.

I know the rules of field work
and refrain from interfering
with the natural order of things
even as I look on like a boxing fan
who has placed a heavy bet
on the underdog.

I quell the urge to run into the fray,
flapping my own arms
like the penguin's ungainly limbs.
Grinding my teeth,
I swallow the urge to shout
Shoo . . . shooooo . . . get away!

The ornithologist stands to my right,
a cool eye studying the scene, taking notes.
She is here in the service of science.
"How do you not take sides?" I ask.
She looks up from her clipboard and replies,
"Even the Skua needs to feed her young."

Rocking the Boat

This must be the boat my mother warned me about—
The one she told me not to rock,
The one that could be tipped over with the wrong word
at the wrong moment.

We are drifting through a labyrinth of blue ice.
The Zodiac's pilot turns off the engine.
He knows when to engage
and when to let the current simply carry us.
He understands the rhythm of resistance and surrender
and allows us to be buffeted lightly by the frozen blocks
that scrape the hull nudging us gently forward.

Twelve of us huddle in the boat oblivious to the cold,
lulled by the peaceful rocking of the small craft.
Beyond the mosaic of ice, a pair of penguins
darts through the open water,
up and down like a needle on a sewing machine
stitching sea and sky together.

In the bow an incessant chatter has begun.
Four passengers compare complaints
about miserable flights,
cramped cabins and spotty internet.
Fifty yards from the boat
a Humpback whale lifts its colossal head
and releases a plume of spray.

The ceaseless yammering drones on
as we drift past cathedrals of ice
where wind-carved caves cast blue shadows
on the shimmering surface.

When I can't take it anymore,
I step gingerly into their circle,
resisting my mother's age-old warnings,
not knowing what I will say until I say it.
"I wonder if you would mind tabling
this conversation until lunch.
This is a sacred place."
They mumble an apology followed by stunned silence.
The boat rocks slightly but stays afloat.
I say thank you
and return to my place.

The Captain's Portrait

for Chelsea Claus

The ship's photographer is oblivious to the onlookers
gathered in the lounge for the ocean view.
She is only aware of her mission
as she deftly directs the man in the navy-blue uniform
to lower his right shoulder, breathe, relax.

She knows a portrait is not a picture,
but a biography. In a single image
she must tell the story of his life.
She steps closer to adjust his sleeve,
smooth out the gold stripes and epaulettes
that tell only part of the tale.

She takes a few practice shots
while respectfully issuing
the subtlest of commands.
Relax your left elbow.
Sit comfortably. Breathe.

Unaccustomed to receiving orders,
he is ill at ease, unwilling or unable
to soften the rigid line of his posture,
the firm set of his jaw,
the direct gaze into the lens.

Now look out to sea,
beyond the swelling white caps
that will not appear in the portrait.
As he complies, the image shifts.
He sees twenty years of Antarctic voyages—
floating mountaintops of icebergs,
Humpback whales breaking the waves,
albatross gliding on currents in the ship's wake.

His breath in sync with the waves now,
he surrenders to the horizon.
She waits while he immerses himself
in the story she has come to tell.
Then with a decisive click of the shutter,
the portrait is complete.

Blue

I thought I knew what blue was
when I flipped through dozens
of paint chips to choose the color
for our bedroom walls.

I thought I knew what blue was
when I stood on the beach at Waikiki
entranced by the sequined water
sparkling in the sunlight.

I was sure I knew what blue was
when I stood under the vaulted ceiling
of St. Chapelle where light poured
through the stained glass like a crystal waterfall.

Yes, I thought I knew what blue was.
Could name every shade in the Pantone Book—
indigo and azure, cerulean and sapphire.
But I had never seen blue until I came here

and saw the ribbon of shimmering shadow
just below the hem of an iceberg
glistening beneath the clear-as-glass
waters of Paradise Bay.

A Day Without a Camera

Morning cruise on Paradise Bay.
Blue and white seascape
like a Tiffany gift box
bearing a gem unlike any other.

Red parka, life jacket
waterproof pants and boots.
All the accoutrements of a morning cruise
on the motorized tender boat.
All but the camera that I left behind
as a pledge to be present
while the boat glides
over the ice-laced bay.

Liberated from the lens,
I abandon the compulsion to capture images,
choosing instead to let them capture me.
Then I spot a Weddell Seal
grinning from an ice floe.
I swear she is posing for us.
Curious and serene,
she lifts her head for a better view.

After a reflexive reach
for the absent camera that itches
like a phantom limb,
I study every detail—
upturned curve of body
flippers folded over belly,
dark eyes piercing the white landscape.
I engrave the image into memory
with a promise to never forget.

Sonnet for a Nameless Iceberg

They call it A-68—
innocuous label for an iceberg
the size of Connecticut,
trillions of tons sheared off
the Larson Ice Shelf,
adrift on the Southern Ocean.

A-68 sounds more like a game—
a mistake made by a Bingo caller.
Oops! he says, correcting himself
to the delight of the lady
who leaps up shouting "I win!"
and races to collect her prize.

If only every mistake were that easy to fix—
Every game that easy to win.

At Sea

The bulletin board in the lobby
announces our location at all times.

You are here

it declares,
naming exotic ports of call
across the Southern Hemisphere.

But now
in this hour before dawn,
it offers only the vaguest hint.

At Sea

as if that is all I need to know.

I have been at sea before
buffeted by waves of confusion—
always with the implied antecedent

Lost

What sea
rocks the ship
in this hour before dawn?

What can I see
when there is no moon, no horizon,
only darkness pressing in from above and below?

What can't I see
looming beyond the bow
in these unnamed waters?

What do I see at sea
in this hour before dawn?
Uncharted. Untethered. Unlimited.

I am here.

That is all I need to know.
At sea.
In this hour before dawn.

Beacon at the Bottom of the World

Arctowski Lighthouse pierces the frozen darkness
just seventy-five miles north of the Antarctic Peninsula.
They say its light is visible for eight nautical miles
penetrating the darkest darkness on Earth
where the black sky and the black waters
swallow the horizon for six months of the year.
Its beam stitches a seam of light across glaciers
that glitter briefly under its slow-motion pirouette,
illuminating a sea where no ships dare to pass
during the long night of the Austral winter.
Although I will never see its night-piercing beacon,
it warms me to think that even there,
at the ice-bound bottom of the world
a light shines in the darkness.

Rookery, The Falklands

A Black-browed Albatross glides
above the tussock grass
that hides the rookery
where a new generation occupies
pedestal nests of mud and feathers.

We trek single file through
the chin-high grass
on a muddy trail
narrow as a snake
and just as treacherous,
strewn with roots and rocks
that slide under foot.

Up ahead, the click of beaks
tap like knitting needles
as we part the curtain of grass
and peer into the nursery.

Their eyes, onyx beads,
lined like Cleopatra's,
meet our gaze briefly
without even a hint
of curiosity.

Perched in their own territory,
they are indifferent to
our mute amazement
while Rockhopper penguins
accompany them
like goth babysitters
in spiked haircuts.

Even when the Caracara vulture
perches imperiously on a rock
in the middle of the colony,
the chicks remain composed
knowing they have nothing to fear.

Soon they will fledge,
soaring like their parents
over the Southern Ocean,
darting in the currents behind
the sterns of passing ships,
wheeling and diving
with infinite grace
for weeks on end.

Inventory

Toothbrush
  Disposable razor
    Hotel shampoo bottle
      Dental floss
        Lipstick tube
          Disposable lighter
            Condoms
              Enema bottle
                Tampon applicator

        No, this is not my bathroom junk drawer.

This is the litany of debris
swallowed by a Black-browed Albatross
who soars above the churning waters
in search of food for her young.
These are the stomach contents
of chicks lying dead on the beach
long before their massive wings
could ever grace the horizon
above the Southern Ocean.

Core Values

Ask any scientist camped out
on the ice for weeks at a time
and they will tell you.
It's all about drilling down.

The deeper you go,
the more you learn.
Time has a way of freezing
the story of our lives.

Here on this distant continent,
what is frozen tells us
who we are,
what we come from,
what we stand to lose.

Imagine,

a single air bubble in a pillar of ice
a mile below the surface,
a whole history of the planet
enshrined for millenia
at the bottom of the earth.

Drill down.

See what you can find
at your own deepest core.
Discover what is frozen
in those places
you never thought
you could reach.

To Dream of Antarctica

Every night I beg my subconscious
to just meet me half-way,
to put me on the prow of a ship
pointing south—I mean True South—
to the pole at the bottom of the Earth
where the icebound world
is both inviting and forbidding.

As I drift into slumber,
I want to be carried
on the arched wings of an albatross
swooping above the wild currents
of the Drake Passage
even if I wake feeling
seasick from the ride.

I want morning to find me
huddled under my summer blanket,
my teeth chattering from the imaginary cold
even as the morning sun penetrates
the windowpane.

Why can't dreams be housed
in a psychic jukebox
with a coin slot to conjure
the same reverie over and over
like a song you know by heart?

The World Without Us

I have seen it, you know. And it is beautiful.
Infinite blue sky alive with Petrels and Albatross.
Endless blue water swarming with iridescent krill.
A continent some think desolate
brims with life at its most resilient.
Over eight million Chinstrap penguins,
and not a single politician, Starbucks, or bank.
If someone asked you to imagine
the world without us,
you might think it empty and grim,
but the whales in Paradise Bay would beg to differ.
and the elephant seals lounging
on the beach at Half-Moon Island
would snore contentedly and never miss us.

Treaty

The Antarctic Treaty, signed by 12 nations in 1959, now includes 54 signatories. The treaty will expire in 2041.

Antarctica has no seat
at the General Assembly.
No ambassador.
No citizenry.
No one with a passport
singing a national anthem
and brandishing a flag.

Antarctica is the schoolyard
where the kindergarten teacher
sent her pupils at recess and said,
"Go play nice with each other,"
And they did . . .
. . . in the name of science,
. . . in the name of nature,
. . . in the name of peace.

Antarctica is the real
United Nations.
Fifty-four of them,
signatories on a treaty
vowing cooperation,
No military presence,
No exploitation of resources,
No boundary lines.

But recess will be over soon.

What will happen when all those countries
who played nice for so long
must decide what's next . . .
. . . in the name of science?
. . . in the name of nature?
. . . in the name of peace?

About the Author

Gloria Heffernan's *Exploring Poetry of Presence* (Back Porch Productions) won the 2021 Central New York Book Award for Nonfiction. She also won the 2022 Naugatuck River Review's Narrative Poetry Prize. Gloria is the author of the poetry collection *What the Gratitude List Said to the Bucket List* (New York Quarterly Books) and the chapbooks *Some of Our Parts* (Finishing Line Press) and *Hail to the Symptom* (Moonstone Press). Her work has appeared in over 100 publications including the anthology *Poetry of Presence (vol. 2)*.

Gloria teaches at the YMCA's Downtown Writers Center in Syracuse NY. She conducts workshops on a variety of topics including *Poetry as a Spiritual Practice*. She lives in Syracuse with her husband and fellow traveler, Jim, and their dog Rosie.

To learn more, visit: www.gloriaheffernan.wordpress.com.

www.ingramcontent.com/pod-product-compliance
Lightning Source LLC
Chambersburg PA
CBHW070942160426
43193CB00011B/1773